DATE DUE

SHOES for Everyone

A Story about Jan Matzeliger

by Barbara Mitchell
illustrations by Hetty Mitchell

A Carolrhoda Creative Minds Book

Carolrhoda Books, Inc./Minneapolis

For Susan Pearson, who gave me her shoes and much more

The author wishes to thank the First Church of Christ in Lynn, Massachusetts, and especially Robert Steele, archivist, for providing her with invaluable source material for the story of this talented inventor.

This book is available in two editions:
Library binding by Carolrhoda Books, Inc.
Soft cover by First Avenue Editions
c/o The Lerner Group
241 First Avenue North
Minneapolis, Minnesota 55401

LIBRARY OF CONGRESS CATALOGING-IN-PUBLICATION DATA

Mitchell, Barbara, 1941-
Shoes for everyone.

(A Carolrhoda creative minds book)
Summary: A biography of the half-Dutch/half-black Surinamese man who, despite the hardships and prejudice he found in his new Massachusetts home, invented a shoe-lasting machine that revolutionized the shoe industry in the late nineteenth century.
1. Matzeliger, Jan Ernst, d. 1889—Juvenile literature. 2. Shoe industry—United States—Biography—Juvenile literature. 3. Afro-American inventors—United States—Biography—Juvenile literature. [1. Matzeliger, Jan Ernst, d. 1889. 2. Inventors. 3. Shoe industry—Biography. 4. Afro-Americans—Biography] I. Mitchell, Hetty, ill. II. Title. III. Series
TS990.M335M58 1986 658'.31'0028 [B] [92] 86-4157
ISBN 0-87614-290-0 (lib. bdg.)
ISBN 0-87614-473-3 (pbk.)

Manufactured in the United States of America
10 11 12 13 14 15 – P/MA – 01 00 99 98 97 96

Table of Contents

AUTHOR'S NOTE

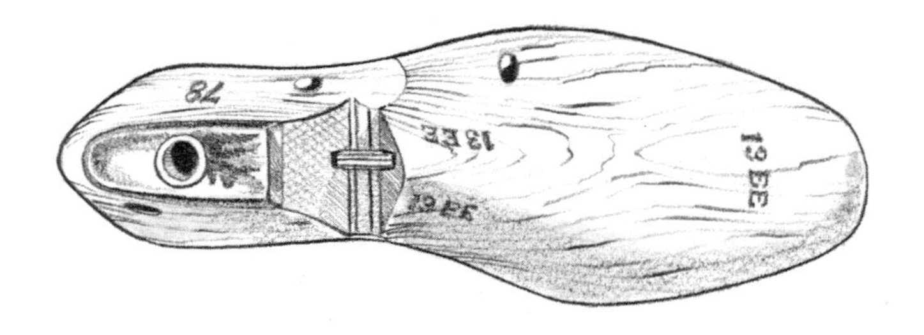

Tucked into the archives of a very old New England church are the pieces of the puzzle that make up the life story of inventor Jan Ernst Matzeliger. Unfortunately, the puzzle is incomplete. Very little is known about Jan's childhood in Dutch Guiana. The name of his mother and the name of the aunt who raised him are lost in history. Equally little is known about the years he spent in Philadelphia.

There is a reason for this scarcity of information about the man who revolutionized the shoe industry. Jan Matzeliger lived at a time when members of the black race were looked down upon and thought to be unimportant. In fact, if he had invented his shoe-lasting machine just 18 years earlier, he would not even have been able to apply for a patent on it. Before the abolishment of slavery, black inventors either had to seek a patent in the name of a white person or conceal their identity. Because Matzeliger lived during this time of prejudice, many of his accomplishments were never written about.

Chapter One

Paramaribo in 1862 was a little piece of Holland, plucked out of Europe and dropped onto the northeast coast of South America. Red tile roofs topped the city's gingerbreadlike houses. The houses were built of brick that had been carried across the sea as ballast on Dutch sailing ships. Inside, the houses were furnished with rich, dark wood, soft carpeting, and priceless heirlooms imported from the homeland. The Dutchmen who had settled Dutch Guiana (called Suriname now) came from Holland's finest families.

Dikes and seawalls hugged the land. Much of this tropical colony—located on the banks of a river just 12 miles from the sea—was at or below sea level. "They will never do it," said those who had stayed at home when the colonists declared that they intended to reclaim their new home from the sea. But the determined Dutchmen, together with some 300,000 slaves brought from West Africa, *had* done it. Slaves had built the sturdy dikes and seawalls. Slaves had cultivated the 800 sugar and rice plantations. Blacks outnumbered the Dutchmen in Dutch Guiana 14 to 1. Paramaribo's marketplace was a rainbow of faces—black, brown, tan, and white—all jostled together in this colorful land.

Market closed at noon in Paramaribo. *Everything* came to a stop there at midday. Paramaribo was very close to the equator, and working in the fierce noontime heat was next to impossible. The market vendors shut down their stalls. The sugarcane cutters laid down their knives. Workers in the government machine shops turned off their whirring machines and headed for the shade.

Jan Matzeliger was only 10, but already he was one of the workers. Papa supervised a machine shop and had put Jan on as an apprentice. "The boy shows real talent," Papa had said proudly. "He's sure to make a first-rate machinist some day."

Jan had many years of his apprenticeship to serve before he would be a machinist. Machining was a highly skilled trade. Learning to cut and shape metal on the fast-turning lathe and other power-operated machines in Papa's shop took all the patience and concentration Jan could muster. He was glad for the noontime break each day. The sun beating hot on Paramaribo's red tile rooftops did not bother Jan. This was his time for strolling down to the river.

The river was a wonderful place. Sawbills, kingfishers, and oil birds strutted along the docks. Clouds of blue butterflies flitted over piles of overripe bananas. Monkeys climbed the seaside almond trees looking for nuts. Jan did not come to see birds or butterflies or monkeys, though. He came to see the ships. Paramaribo's river docks were nearly always lined with steamships. "Where do they go, Papa?" Jan had asked on their early visits to the river front.

"Out to the sea, son, and around the world," Papa had said.

The ships at the docks were merchant ships.

They carried sugar and coffee and precious spices to faraway lands. Today there was a hide ship in. The hide ships carried their cargo to North America, to the New England shoe factories there. Then they came back to Paramaribo loaded with bundles of cloth from the New England mills—and with barrels of shoes.

Jan stood fascinated as a seaman unloaded a barrel packed tight with these northern wonders neatly tied in pairs. Shoes were special. Jan got a new pair of leather ones each time he outgrew his old ones. That was because Papa had more money than most. Boys who worked along the docks wore wooden shoes. Many Paramaribo boys had no shoes at all; shoes were costly.

The sun was high overhead now. His aunt would have dinner ready, Jan realized. He turned reluctantly from the shouting seamen and headed for the house on Aunt's tree-lined street. Aunt lived on the most elegant street in town. Orange trees, royal palms, and tamarinds lined the walkway that led to her stately home.

Papa was already seated and Aunt was serving the food when Jan slipped into his chair in the flower-filled dining room. "There was a hide ship in," he said by way of explanation.

Jan's aunt smiled and handed him his plate. Her brother's son had his father's love of the sea. All the Dutch loved the sea, she often said.

Papa was a Dutchman. He had been sent out by the Dutch government to manage their machine shops in the colony. Mama was a black Surinamese, but Jan did not remember much about her. He had lived with his aunt since he was three.

"You have your Mama's warm brown eyes," Aunt would often say to Jan. Both the West African and the Dutch could be seen in Jan. His skin was the color of the rich, creamy coffee Aunt drank from the china cups with the blue windmills on them.

Jan stirred his plate of shrimp and rice thoughtfully. "Someday I am going to get on one of those ships and sail around the world," he said.

When Jan was 19, he did just that. He came in to dinner one noon with the news that he had signed on as a seaman with the Dutch East Indies Company. Aunt was upset. She did not like to see the handsome young man she had raised taking off for heaven knew where.

"It is for the best," Papa said. "A fine machinist like Jan will have greater opportunities in Europe, or perhaps in North America." True to his father's prediction, Jan had developed into an outstanding machinist.

The day came when it was time for Jan to ship out. Aunt handed him a small memento of home, a jar of green nutmegs and coffee beans preserved in alcohol. Jan tucked the little jar into his sea-bag. "I shall keep it always." he said. Both he and Aunt knew he might never return to Paramaribo.

No sooner did the great steamship put out to sea than it developed engine trouble. "I know a bit about machines, Sir," Jan told the officer in charge of the engine room. Soon the ship was sailing smoothly on its way.

"Get young Matzeliger down there," the captain ordered whenever the engines began to cough and sputter.

Jan spent two years sailing to the Far East. Then his ship set out for North America. On a crisp day in 1873, they docked in Philadelphia, a hustling, bustling port city. Merchants along Front and Second streets haggled over cargo from India, China, and the Mediterranean. Even more exciting to Jan were the many busy factories he saw—all of them full of machines. William Cramp & Sons Shipbuilders was turning out sturdy iron steamships. The great Baldwin Locomotive Works was building huge huffing-puffing engines. There ought to be some fine opportunities for a machinist here, Jan thought. Jan decided he had had enough of sailing around the world, so he signed out of the Dutch East Indies Company and left his ship.

Making it understood that he wanted a job as a machinist would not be easy in Philadelphia.

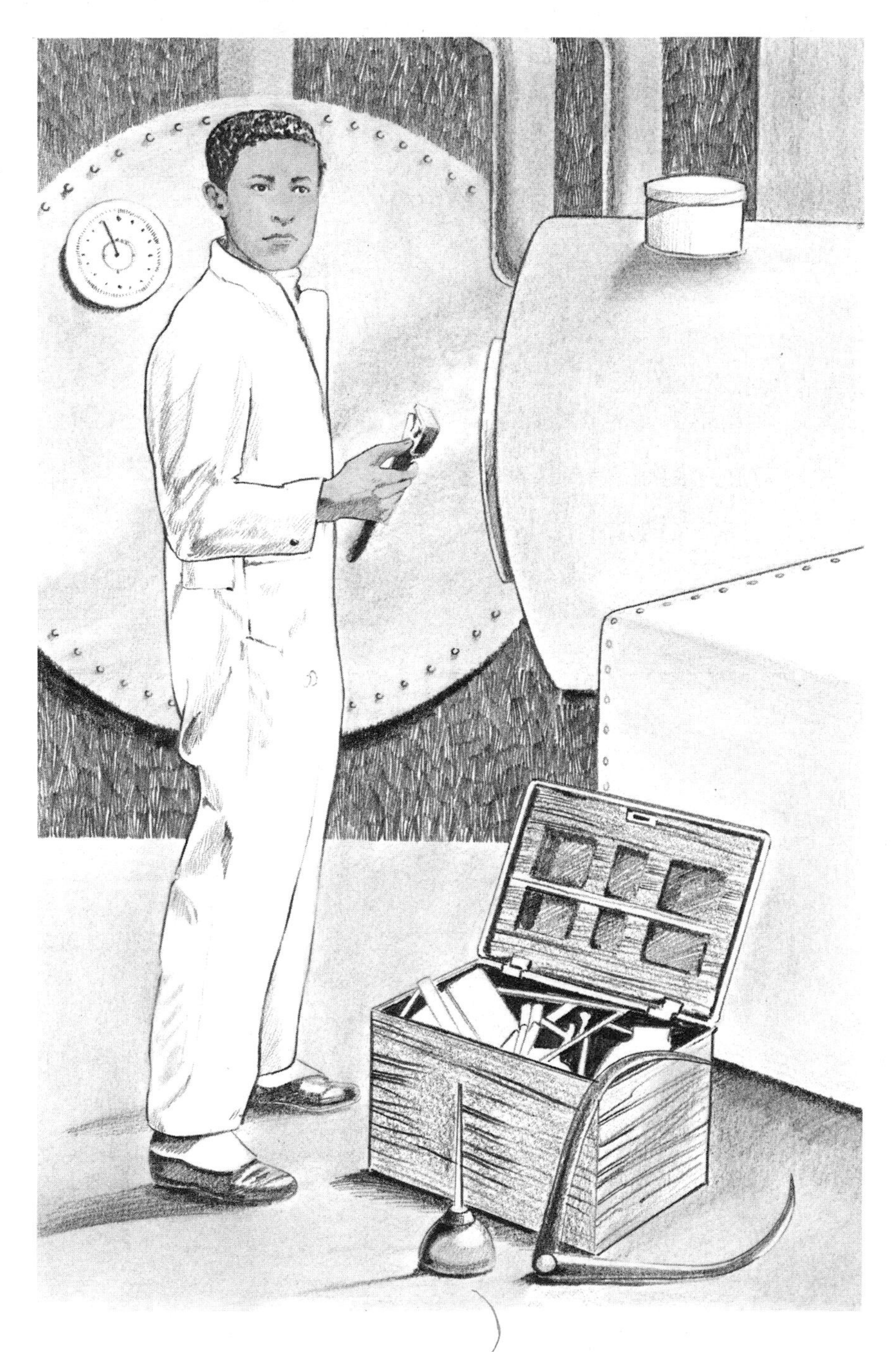

He knew very little English. Dutch was the official language in Paramaribo and on his Dutch-owned ship, too. He went from machine shop to machine shop, showing by gestures and with halting speech that he wanted to go inside to demonstrate his skills. He soon found, however, that door after door was shut firmly in his face, often before he could say even a word or two.

Chapter Two

Jan took a walk around the city. He saw black stevedores unloading Philadelphia's ships. Black street cleaners were sweeping Philadelphia's cobblestones. Black women scrubbed the sparkling marblestone doorsteps and polished the shiny brass knockers on Walnut Street. Black liverymen handed smartly dressed ladies down from carriages on Chestnut Street. Black porters met Philadelphia's trains. The truth of it all was suddenly clear to Jan. In all those machine shops, Jan had not seen one black worker. Not knowing English had not been the problem at all. The problem was that skilled jobs did not go to blacks in Philadelphia. The foremen answering the doors Jan knocked on had taken one look at this sailor with the coffee-colored skin and turned him away. Most of their men simply refused to work alongside a black man.

Jan kept on walking. The crisp afternoon turned dark and chill. Black cooks were darting in and out of alleyways leading to good-smelling kitchens. Black butlers were handing around silver trays in softly lit windows. But nowhere did he see a black person dining. Where did a hungry black seaman go for something to eat, Jan wondered. He headed down Spruce Street. Out of the evening stillness came the sound of singing.

The rich, rhythmic music suddenly reminded Jan of home. He followed his ears. The comforting sound led him to the door of a church. It was just a little church, and it was filled to the bursting point. In its center, a stove sent out a warming glow. Black hands drew him in. Friendly voices gave him a hearty welcome. Up from the basement there drifted the smell of hot food. Jan had discovered the hub of Philadelphia's black community—the church.

After a hot meal, Jan poured out his job-hunting story, partly in English, partly in Dutch.

His new friends nodded knowingly. Despite Jan's halting English, they understood the situation all too well. They could find him a place on the street-cleaning crew, or perhaps working in the sewers, they said.

"But I am a *machinist*," Jan finished.

His listeners shook their heads. Jan's skills did not matter to employers in this city that was fast filling up with former slaves.

Philadelphia was the first city north of the "freedom line." Just eight years before Jan's arrival, Philadelphia Quakers had still been smuggling escaped slaves into the city from Wilmington, Delaware, the last stop on the Underground Railroad. When slaves crossed over the Delaware-Pennsylvania line, they were in free territory. While some former slaves had gone on to Canada, many had chosen to stay in Philadelphia. Now, after the end of the Civil War and with the abolishment of slavery, they were sending for freed relatives to join them.

Jobs—like schools, churches, and housing—were segregated in Philadelphia during the 1870s. The job market was pretty well sewn up. The Irish had taken over the bricklaying and bridge-building trades. The Italians had become the street vendors and tailors. The Jewish population controlled the garment industry and neighborhood shops. White workers did not want the new black citizens taking over the few remaining available jobs that required skilled labor. These new blacks should "know their place," said the white workers.

There was nothing for Jan to do but work at odd jobs. In his off hours, he continued to explore this city in which he was definitely a member of a minority race. Although Philadelphia had the largest population of any American city in 1873, blacks still made up only four percent of the citizenry. Blacks were not welcome at the theater or at the opera house. Although a law had recently been passed allowing blacks to ride the streetcars, Jan was met with cold stares whenever he chose to ride and was forced to move to the rear of the car.

On one of his explorations, he came upon a tiny shop tucked away on a side street. The sign over the door showed a leather shoe. The little painted shoe brought to mind the happy childhood memory of barrels of shoes piled on the docks of friendly Paramaribo. Jan opened the door and went inside the shop. Shoes in various stages of repair were everywhere. In their midst sat a shoemaker quietly going about his delicate work. At his fingertips sat something dear to Jan's heart—a machine.

As if by magic, this small wonder of a machine

was sewing the seam of a shoe sole beneath the shoemaker's hands. Jan had never seen anything like it. "It's a McKay sole-sewing machine," the shoemaker informed his fascinated visitor. Something about the young man's intense interest touched the heart of the shoemaker. Jan soon had himself a new job—a job with a machine.

This new apprentice was no ordinary worker; the shoemaker could see that. Jan quickly became skilled at operating the McKay machine, and his fascination with the shoe-making process was endless. "If you really want to learn about the machines that make shoes, you ought to go to Lynn," the shoemaker told Jan after they had worked together for some two years.

Lynn, Massachusetts, was the shoe manufacturing center of North America. Most of the town's workers were involved in its flourishing shoe industry, which made over half of the shoes in the United States. The best workers in the trade had trained there since colonial days. Jan began to think about going to Lynn in order to learn more about shoemaking.

Chapter Three

Jan soon decided to leave Philadelphia. He arrived in Lynn, Massachusetts, on a raw winter day in 1877. Philadelphia weather may have been crisp, but Lynn was just plain cold. Columns of smoke from the factories shot up into a steel gray sky. The winds whipping up from nearby Boston Harbor sent a chill through Jan's South American bones. He knew where to go to find a warm welcome in a new city this time, though. During the years he had spent in Philadelphia, he had become a devoted Christian. When he had left, his church friends had given him a shiny new silver lapel pin that read, "Safe in Jesus." On his first Sunday in Lynn, he brushed his suit off, put on his new pin, and went off to church.

As it turned out, there was no black church in town. Unlike Philadelphia with its 25 black churches, Lynn was not close to the freedom line and did not have a large enough black community to support even one black church. No matter, Jan thought. A church is a church, isn't it? He went into a white church and sat down. No welcoming hands reached out to take his. No warm voices bid him good morning. He was greeted with stares as cold as the winds off Boston Harbor.

The next Sunday, he tried another church and received the same chilly reception. On the third Sunday, he tried still another church and found that he was no more welcome there than in the first two churches. In the meantime, he had set about looking for work in the shoe industry. Things were not going much better there than they had in the churches.

Lynn was full of immigrants looking for work in its thriving shoe industry. Some companies, eager for workers, even had primers made up in simple English to help these immigrants learn their jobs. Still, when Jan went from factory to factory, he was turned down at every one. The shoemen looked with suspicion at Jan.

Could a black man learn to make shoes as well as an Irishman or an Italian? They had their doubts. "Sorry, we have no openings," they all said.

Jan Matzeliger was not one to give up. He had come to this town to learn about shoe machinery, and he was going to do it, even if he had to visit every shoe factory in Lynn—and there were 170 of them.

After days of walking the streets, Jan came to the Harney Brothers factory. Mr. Harney took a long, hard look at him. "You say you've had experience on the McKay?" he said at last.

"Yes, in Philadelphia," Jan replied.

"Might just as well give you a try," Mr. Harney said. He was in need of sewers.

Jan's deft fingers went to work on one of Harney Brothers' McKay sole-sewing machines. He handed his observer the finished sole.

Mr. Harney turned the sole over and over in his hands. The stitches were straight and even. The sole was perfectly sewn. It took most new workers weeks of training before they could turn out a piece of work like this. "Young man, you are hired," the astonished shoe manufacturer said.

Jan spent his days sewing soles. At night he went to school to improve what little English he had picked up in Philadelphia. He was soon speaking the language fluently. After paying his room and board, he spent what was left of his small salary on books. He had discovered a wonderful set, called *Science for Everyone*, in a secondhand shop. It became the start of his library of books on mechanical science and physics. Jan was becoming more and more fascinated by machines and wanted to learn as much as he could about them.

Jan often walked past a particular secondhand shop. In the window was something that he dearly wanted—a set of drawing instruments. The delicate little instruments used by draftsmen to design machines were expensive, even secondhand. Still, Jan made up his mind to save until he could afford to buy them. Whirling about in his mind were dozens of ideas for new kinds of machines.

The day he brought the drawing instruments home at last was his happiest since coming to Lynn. He took the tools out of their worn case and went right to work. His drawing papers soon showed wondrous things—an orange-wrapping

machine, a railroad car coupler, a one-piece toggle spear for fishing. Jan dreamed of the day when he would have enough money to turn the ideas on paper into real working machines.

There was ample opportunity for Jan to learn about machines in the Harney Brothers factory. Machines had taken over the shoe industry. Each worker had his or her own part of the shoe to make and the machine to do it. There were machines for upper work. There were machines for stock fitting and bottoming. There were buttonholing machines and buffing machines. The whole process hummed merrily along until it came to the lasting. Then everything came to a stop.

Lasting—connecting the upper part of the shoe to the inner sole—was a complicated process. The fit, the walking ease, and the look of the shoe all depended upon the quality of the lasting. Stretching the leather over the *last* (a wooden model of the foot) took great skill, and tacking the finished shape into place was just as tricky. Try as they might, no one had been able to come up with a machine that could do such things, so the people who were the lasters still worked by hand. They were the kings of the shoemaking trade, and they let their power be known. "This business would be nothing without us," they boasted.

Some days the lasters were not able to keep up with the machines. Some days they chose not to keep up. They had a strong union that kept the number of apprentices down and guaranteed their jobs. Time after time, Jan came into work to find his co-workers sitting around waiting on the "kings." "The lasters are behind again . . . no more work for a week . . . the lasters are on strike again," he heard time after time.

"I can make a machine that would do their job perfectly," Jan said quietly one day.

His co-workers exchanged glances. "*Sure* you can," they said. This would make good talk for the lunch break.

In no time at all, the comment had reached the lasters. They found Jan's claim very amusing. "Make a machine that can turn a shoe and tack it? Make a machine that knows when to *stop* turning a shoe!" they said.

"No man can make a machine that will do these things—unless he can make a machine that has fingers," one old laster said. The other lasters laughed heartily.

What none of them knew was that Jan Matzeliger was dead serious. He had been drawing up ideas for a machine that could do everything the lasters thought was impossible. They also did not know that once Jan Matzeliger made up his mind to do something, he did it.

The first thing Jan did after his startling announcement was to go and see his boss. "I would like to suggest that you make me millwright," he said.

As millwright, it would be Jan's job to circulate about the entire factory, checking all machines for needed parts and repairs. It would give him an opportunity to watch the lasters at work.

His boss looked at him thoughtfully. It was not a bad idea. Anytime a machine was down, it was Matzeliger who knew how to get it back into working order. "The job is all yours," he said.

Now Jan was roaming the factory daily, and his sharp eyes took in every movement of the lasters' strong, skillful hands. When he had memorized their technique, he rented a room over the old West Lynn Mission so that he could work on his invention in secret. There were other workers in the shoe industry trying to come up with a lasting machine, and Jan could not risk having

his idea stolen. The old West Lynn Mission was a shabby little building in a poor section of town. It had no heat, but the rent was cheap. Jan needed to save every penny he could for his invention. The chilly room was soon filled with his drawings; the problem he had before him had no simple solution.

Jan kept sketching as spring turned to summer, and the stacks of drawings grew higher and higher. None of them seemed to work. Night after night, when he was too tired to draw any longer, Jan lay awake thinking. *Was* he trying to do the impossible after all? In the morning he would get up and draw before going to work all day at the shoe factory. Then, as soon as he got home, he would go back to his drawing board.

By the fall of 1880, he had made a model. It was nothing more than old cigar boxes strung up with wire and nails and pieces of scrap wood—but it would work! Jan was almost sure of it. Late one night he heard a tap at his secret workshop door. It was another inventor; news of what Jan was doing had leaked out after all. The inventor took the crude cigar-box model in his hands. He turned it over and over, studying it. "I'll give you $50 for it," he said.

Fifty dollars. I could buy some tools and really get down to work with that, Jan thought. But if this other inventor thinks enough of a cardboard model to pay $50 for it, I must be on the right track.

"I am sorry. The model is not for sale," Jan said.

Still, a cigar-box model would not last any shoes. What he needed now was a real working model, a model made of metal. Jan began to spend his free hours scouring the junkyards and factory cast-off heaps of Lynn.

Jan's explorations turned up some wonderful finds—bits of scrap metal and parts of old broken-down machines. There were some things, though, that just could not be found because Jan had invented them. He could not afford to pay someone to make them, either. Somehow he would have to make them himself, he realized with a sinking heart. Shaping new parts from metal would require a forge for heating the metal (to make it bendable) and a lathe for shaping the warm metal.

Forges and lathes were expensive pieces of equipment. They did not simply turn up in junkyards. Jan longed for the well-equipped

machine shop back in Paramaribo. Deeply discouraged, he took his problem to his boss, who listened sympathetically. Harney Brothers had no forge Jan could use, but the Beal Brothers shoe factory did, he said.

Chapter Four

For the sake of his invention, Jan left his job at Harney Brothers and went to work at Beal Brothers. His new employer gave him floor space and the use of their old forge and lathe. Jan partitioned off his workspace and got to work on his metal model.

News of what was going on in the secret workspace during the new employee's off-hours got around. "A *machine* that can last shoes!" the factory workers said. They spent their time circulating cruel jokes about Jan Matzeliger.

The going was slow for Jan. The old lathe he had been loaned was barely workable. Often the worn-out pieces of metal he refashioned fell apart in his hands after many grueling hours of work on them. The months turned into a year, then another year. For the first time in his life, Jan Matzeliger felt like giving up.

Somehow he had to get the money for better materials. He cut his food allowance to 5¢ a day. He took a part-time job driving coachloads of young people out to Raddin's Grove, a recreation area by the Saugus River.

The young woman who ran the refreshment stand at the park took special notice of Jan. The popular coach driver was always cheerful and pleasant with his young passengers, but after they had gone off, the dejected look would return to his face.

One night she thought that the coachman looked especially tired. She was sure he had grown thinner in the months that she had been watching him.

"Would you care for a refreshment?" she asked Jan.

Jan shook his head. "Not tonight," he said.

He did not have the money to pay for anything.

Enna Jordan sensed as much. Enna was a buttonholer in the shoe factory in addition to her work at the park. She had heard about Jan Matzeliger and his secret workshop—and about his money troubles. She would not hurt his pride by offering a refreshment without payment. She made up her mind to invite him to supper the next week instead.

"He is always so alone," she said to her friend Bessie Lee.

Bessie Lee agreed. She was a buttonholer too and had observed Jan at the factory. "He is always so friendly," she said, "but he has no friends. I think we should invite him to Christian Endeavor."

Christian Endeavor was the young peoples' group at Lynn's North Congregational Church. The fun-loving group was just what Jan needed. He was soon caught up in skating parties, theater productions, and after-church get togethers. Best of all were the Bible study hours. Jan had a passion for Bible study, and he missed the fellowship of his old Philadelphia church. The activities and companionship all added up to the encouragement he needed to go on with his lasting machine.

One day, after returning from her noon break, Enna found a handmade leather lunch pail on her buttonhole machine. "I noticed you carried your lunch in a paper sack," Jan told her. It was his way of thanking her for the help she had given him.

By 1882 Jan had his scrap-metal model completed. Another hopeful inventor paid him a visit. "I'll give you $1,500 just for the part that turns the leather around the toe," he said.

Now Jan knew he had the whole machine figured out. "The machine is not for sale in parts," he said.

As soon as the curious inventor had left, Jan took the parts of a shoe and put his model to a final test. The little wonder of a machine shaped and turned and tacked beautifully. There was just one problem. A scrap-metal machine would not hold up to factory testing. What use would it be to receive a patent for his invention only to have the machine fail in the end? A government grant to make, use, and sell an undependable version of his machine would be pointless. What he needed now was a good model, a model made of all new parts and with real precision—an expensive machine.

Chapter Five

Now Jan spent all his free time knocking on the doors of Lynn businessmen, hoping to convince them to put money into his invention. The businessmen listened with little interest. They had heard from these lasting machine fellows before. Why, one businessman had invested $100,000 in one, only to have the inventor's so-called miracle machine fail. The story had gone all over Lynn.

Finally, C.H. Delnow and M.S. Nichols, two Lynn businessmen with money to invest, agreed to back Jan's machine provided he give them a two-thirds interest in any profit that might result. That meant that Jan himself would receive only a third of the money. But he was poorer than ever now and had little choice but to agree to the arrangement or give up on his idea altogether. The Union Lasting Machine Company was formed, and Jan set about making his third model.

Now, with a good model underway, Jan could apply for a patent. Applying for this license from the government meant submitting a set of detailed drawings—seven pages of them, plus eight pages of description. Then came the waiting.

"Any news from Washington?" his friends at North Church asked Sunday after Sunday.

"Nothing," Jan said.

There was more reason than usual for the slow turning of the official wheels. The examiners at the patent office did not know quite what to make of the fat little packet of drawings. First of all, they could not believe the machine could actually do what its inventor claimed it could. "And to tell you the truth," one official confessed, "I simply cannot understand those complicated drawings."

The other officials nodded sheepishly. The drawings were too difficult for them to understand as well. "Still, the man may have something here," one examiner said. At last they decided to send an examiner to Lynn to see the machine itself.

Jan took the official to his machine and sat him down beside it. "Be ready to catch the finished shoe," he said.

The examiner settled back in his chair, hands in pockets.

"Now this will only take but a moment," Jan warned.

Rat-tat-tat-tat. Rat-tat-tat-tat. The machine went to work. It held the last, gripped the leather, drew the leather over the last, fitted the leather at the heel and the toe, moved the last forward, fed the nails, and drove the nails. FLIP! The finished shoe landed in the astonished examiner's lap. It had all taken place in the space of one minute.

On March 20, 1883, Jan Ernst Matzeliger was granted Patent No. 274,207 for his lasting machine. He had done what had seemed impossible—invented a machine that could take the place of human hands. But would a machine that performed such an intricate task hold up under factory conditions?

The crucial test was set for May 29, 1885. Rat-tat-tat-tat. Rat-tat-tat-tat. Jan's smooth-running machine clinked its way through 75 pairs of women's shoes with no trouble at all. Delnow and Nichols were delighted. They wanted to begin manufacturing the machine immediately, but they did not have the kind of money needed for such a large-scale operation. They called upon George W. Brown, the northeast agent for the Wheeler Wilson Sewing Machine Company and Sidney W. Winslow, who later became known as the machinery king of New England. They provided the needed funds—on the condition that they take over Jan's patent on his machine. Once again it was a case of giving in or forgetting about the entire project. Jan ended up receiving a block of stock in the new company, the Consolidated Lasting Machine Company, that was formed as a result of the deal.

The new company went into production. Nearly every shoe manufacturer in Lynn was interested in buying the new machine. A good hand laster could turn out 50 pairs of shoes in a 10-hour day. The new machine could do up to 700 in the same amount of time. A team of 250 workers had to work day and night in a Beverly, Massachusetts, factory to keep up with orders.

Shoe manufacture in New England boomed. Exports to other parts of the world reached a new high. Country after country wanted to adopt this machine that could save time, that could adapt to various shoe styles, and that increased production to such an extent that shoe prices

could be brought down dramatically. People who had never been able to afford shoes before suddenly found them affordable. Jan Matzeliger had quietly revolutionized the shoe industry.

In all the hub-bub, the inventor was practically forgotten. "Invented the 'Nigger Head Machine,' didn't he?" someone would remark from time to time. The lasters, disgruntled at having to go to school to learn how to operate the machine and afraid that it would one day replace them, had given it this cruel name. They had no way of foretelling, of course, that Jan's machine would in the near future bring them more work and easier work than they had ever thought possible.

Jan Matzeliger made few changes in his modest lifestyle. He taught oil painting classes and Sunday school, and he took particular joy in becoming the leader of Christian Endeavor. When young Augustine Manwell, a member of the group, wanted to enter the ministry, it was Jan who paid the boy's way through Amherst College and Seminary.

Jan was an enthusiastic Christian Endeavor leader. The excitement he generated brought more and more young people from the shoe factories out to the meetings. He especially enjoyed promoting the group's grand year-end picnic at Raddin's Grove. The day of the annual outing in the summer of 1886 marked a turning point in Jan's life. The morning dawned gray and threatening. Would an all-day drizzle set in, Jan wondered, or was there, as the Dutch said of a day that was sure to clear off, enough blue in the sky to make a pig a pair of pants?

The morning wore on. Finally it was time to go over to the church and make a decision. Jan looked at the eager faces turned to him. "What are a few raindrops? Of course we'll go," he said.

The picnic was rained out after all. The drenched picnickers all came down with colds. Jan's healthy young charges recovered in no time, but Jan did not. By October he had developed a worrisome cough. "He does not look well at all," L. M. Durgin remarked to his wife. Mr. Durgin was a fellow shoe-laster and a friend of Jan's.

"I know he does not eat as he should," Mrs. Durgin said. The Durgins convinced Jan to come and board with them.

Despite Mrs. Durgin's nursing and her nutritious meals, Jan grew steadily worse. The doctor gave an unhappy diagnosis—Jan Matzeliger had tuberculosis.

So many shoe-factory workers came down with tuberculosis that it was known around Lynn as the "shoemaker's disease." It all came from hunching over workbenches in closed-up factories for most of their lives, the doctors said. People with money went off to sunny sanatoriums and filled their lungs with fresh mountain air. Since Jan did not have that kind of money, the doctor ordered him to the Lynn hospital.

During his long days in the hospital, Jan sketched a fourth, streamlined model of his lasting machine and did watercolors of ships and the sea for his friends. His tired body, worn out from the years of overwork and meager meals, was not able to fight off the disease. On August 24, 1889, Jan Matzeliger died. He was just 37 years old.

In his will, Jan remembered all those who had been close to him. To 15 of his friends, his doctor, and the Lynn hospital, he gave two-thirds of his stock in the Union Lasting Machine Company. The other third of this stock and all of his stock in the Consolidated Lasting Machine Company he gave to North Church. The money was to be used as the pastor saw fit toward the support and comfort of Lynn's poor.

Black children and white children go to school together in Lynn now. Every fall their new shoes make a clatter up and down school stairs. Every spring, wearing scuffed and comfortable shoes, the children of the Sunday school where Jan once taught tread softly down Gentian Path in Pine Grove Cemetery. There they place flowers on the grave of Jan Matzeliger, the man who gave shoes to the world.

AFTERWORD

In 1899, 41 smaller shoe-machine manufacturing companies were merged with the Consolidated Lasting Machine Company to form a New Jersey corporation known as the United Shoe Machine Corporation. Shoe lasting is still done on machines based on Jan Matzeliger's invention. His lasting machine was awarded a gold medal by the Pan American Exhibition in 1901. The American Negro Commemorative Society honored Jan Matzeliger with its twenty-second commemorative medal.

The $10,000 worth of stock willed to North Church enabled the congregation to pay off its mortgage. North Church later merged with First Church to form the First Church of Christ in Lynn. There you can see an original portrait of Jan Matzeliger, tacks from his drawing board, the lunch pail he made for Enna Jordan, and the Bible he willed to Bessie Lee. At the Lee Museum, established by Bessie Lee in Lee, Maine, you can see Jan's drawing instruments and the toys he made for Bessie's nephew. No one knows just what happened to the jar of coffee beans and nutmegs, Jan's parting gift from his aunt that he kept all his life.

In 1976 the citizens of Lynn honored Jan Matzeliger with a day in his memory. In October 1984, the governor of Massachusetts signed into law a measure naming a bridge in Lynn in honor of the inventor. Soon after, the Lynn chapter of the National Association for the Advancement of Colored People (NAACP) began raising funds for a suitable monument to be erected at the base of the bridge.